ANTIBES/GUIDE TO THE PICASSO MUSEUM

DANIÈLE GIRAUDY
Curator of the Museum

HAZAN

Cover illustration: Grimaldi Castle and the Vauban
ramparts photographed from the sea. Photo: Marianne
Greenwood.

Translated by:
Charles Lynn Clark
Graphics:
Xavier Barral
Photocomposition:
Comp'Infor
Photoengraving:
Sele offset, Turin
© 1987 by Fernand Hazan, Paris
© 1987, SPADEM and ADAGP, Paris
Printed in June 1987
by Geraficromo in Cordoda, Spain
ISBN 2 85025 131 3

From Grimaldi Castle to the Picasso Museum

"When we started, we
didn't know what we
were doing. If you had
told me, 'we're going to
make a museum,' I
wouldn't have come. But
you said, 'I've got a studio
for you.' You really didn't
know quite what you
were going to do: that's
why everything turned
out so well, because you
didn't *imitate* a museum."
Picasso

Grimaldi Castle overlooks the ramparts surrounding the oldest part of Antibes. In 1925, the castle, then being used by the French Army Corps of Engineers, was put up for auction. A young classics teacher at the secondary school in Cannes, Romuald de la Souchère, managed to stop the sale; the town of Antibes then agreed to purchase the monument "on the condition that a museum be set up there." Thus did Grimaldi Castle become the Antibes Museum of Art, History, and Archeology in 1928. Dor de la Souchère, the driving force behind the castle's transformation, became the Museum's first curator. He spent ten years reconstructing the town's past with Greek and Roman inscriptions from the Grasse district, medieval parchments, coins, arms, pieces of enamel work, notices from the French Revolution, portraits, and Empire memorabilia... while also overseeing the renovation and conversion of the castle, which was on the verge of falling into ruins. The restoration project was made possible by the support of the town, the "Ligurian Group for Scientific and Archeological Studies of the Antibes Museum," the benefactors whose names have been carved in marble at the entrance to the rooms, and the French Office for Historical Landmarks, which classed the Museum in 1927.

Two particularly important exhibitions allowed the new Museum to enrich its nascent collections: *Portrait of Antibes,* in 1936, brought the Museum the *Aundi Reredos,* a valuable primitive found in an advanced state of neglect. The following year, *Return from Elba* documented a famous episode in the life of Napoleon, which was later developed at the Musée Naval et Napoléonien. During these years, the Curator also organized regular exhibitions on the work of "young and contemporary masters."

In 1946, the Museum's destiny changed course when Dor de la Souchère happened to meet Picasso, accompanied by the recently deceased photographer Michel Sima, at the beach. Picasso and his young companion, Françoise Gilot, had found a place in Golfe-Juan. As their quarters were quite cramped, Picasso was overjoyed by Dor de la Souchère's offer to use part of the castle as a studio, and was soon to be found working there. He spent six months painting in his new studio, and left the Museum nearly everything he did on its premises: the twenty-five paintings that make up the Antipolis Series and forty-four preparatory sketches. When he came back a year later, he added a large panel, *Ulysses and the Sirens.* Thus was the first museum devoted to a living artist born. When he donated his works, the painter stipulated that they never leave the museum premises, and that condition has always been respected. In 1948, a major donation of ceramics that the artist had made in Vallauris — seventy-seven plates, vases, animals, and "tanagras"

"In 1923 (I don't recall what day or month it was) I took the little electric tram that used to run between the peaceful, sun-drenched towns of Cannes and Antibes... When I got off in Antibes, I found myself in front of a big, dilapidated ruin of a building; on the door, there was a sign announcing the 'Auction of the former Army Corps of Engineers Building, known as Antibes Castle.' Meeting the Mayor, I remarked, 'Sir, I've just found out Antibes Castle is up for sale. I do hope you're planning to buy it.'" Monsieur Ardisson, the Mayor of Antibes in 1923, gave Dor de la Souchère, a young teacher he had never met before, a very cautious answer: "I'm afraid we can't afford it."
After Dor de la Souchère managed to convince the appropriate officials in Nice to call off the auctioning of the castle, he was told bluntly: "A museum? It's far too big for that. What on earth would you put in it? Let's be realistic."
Danièle Giraudy, *Picasso à Antibes,* catalogue n° 1.

— was added to the collection of paintings and drawings. Then, in 1950, Picasso decided to make yet another donation and gave the Museum the two large cement statues, made at the Château de Boisgeloup in 1931, that had opened the Spanish Pavilion at the 1937 World Fair in Paris. The works Picasso did during his six-month stay at the castle can be "read" as a diary of his inspiration, for they allow us to retrace the artist's creative processes from day to day (all of the works are dated on the back).

For each painting, there are color notations, preparatory drawings, and sketches that show, step by step, how it evolved. In addition, period photographs record the various stages — simplified states, for the most part — in the elaboration of the paintings. Moreover, recent x-rays clearly reveal what lies "beneath" the finished canvases, and how the artist proceeded in his work. This is the principal attraction and great lesson of the Antipolis Series, displayed in the place of its birth.

For the official inauguration of the Picasso Museum in 1949, Marie Cuttoli, President of the Friends of the Museum, enriched the collections with a donation of engravings, followed later by a group of tapestries. A friend of the painter's, she had invited him to Shady Rock, her Cap d'Antibes estate, in the summer of 1946. She helped Dor de la Souchère in his fundraising efforts and introduced him to friends of hers, painters and sculptors represented in her own collection (Ernst, Calder, Léger...), whose works would later be exhibited in the Museum. Together, Picasso and Marie Cuttoli brought the Museum into the twentieth century: since 1951, the Museum has presented the work of many important contemporary artists — including de Staël, Richier, Atlan, Magnelli, Clavé, Prassinos, Debré, and Hartung — and organized exhibitions around such "Antibes" writers as Audiberti, Kazantzaki, and Prévert.

In 1950, Jean Cocteau and Henri Langlois organized the first *International Festival of the Film of Tomorrow,* designed to complement the young Cannes Festival by screening censured works.

During the first twenty-five years of the Picasso Museum's existence, eighty-five exhibitions enriched the collections with some two hundred paintings donated by the artists themselves. Since 1981, when Danièle Giraudy was named Dor de la Souchère's successor, another two hundred or so works have been acquired by purchase or donation: Miró's *Sea Goddess,* Modigliani's *Portrait of Picasso,* Picabia's *Self-Portrait,* and works Nicolas de Staël painted in Antibes (now on permanent display in the Museum), including *Le Fort-Carré* and his last work, *The Big Concert.* Moreover, additional "Antibes Picassos" from 1946, which had previously been in foreign collections, have been purchased with the help of national, regional, and local organisms, and the generous support of private benefactors.

Today, the Picasso Museum's objectives are to bring together and display works by artists associated with Antibes (e.g., Picasso, Staël, Richier), to encourage young artists by purchasing their works and exhibiting the winners of the Antibes Prize, and to strenghten the links between the castle and the collections by commissioning new works (e.g., the twenty « Homages to Picasso » and sculptures by Poirier and Pagès). Recent innovations include daily workshops for visiting schoolchildren and, for the handicapped, the *Sculpture and Fragance Garden,* installed on the terrace which was once the Acropolis of Antipolis.

It should also be noted that a series of catalogues on the Museum's collections is published by the town of Antibes. In addition to posters, postcards, and slides, some twenty different catalogues are available for purchase by the many visitors the Museum attracts from around the globe.

The Museum is also a place for research and experimentation: young curators regularly come to the Museum for traineeships and seminars; the collections have now been computerized; and travelling exhibitions and exchanges with the Picasso Museums in Paris and Barcelona have been organized.

In 1977, Dor de la Souchère's last exhibition, *Invitation to Oblivion,* brought together the last fifty winners of the "Rome Prize." This was to be the last pirouette of the Picasso Museum's founder — as elegant and fragile as the turtledoves he so loved — before he passed away on December 10, 1977, at age eighty-nine. He had spent fifty years of his life perfecting his masterpiece, the Museum where, as he wrote in 1961, "one becomes a survivor."

Picasso and the Antipolis Series

"I paint the way other
people write their
autobiography. My
canvases, whether
finished or not, are the
pages in my journal..."
Picasso

Picasso's hands, Vallauris, 1954.
Photo: André Villers.

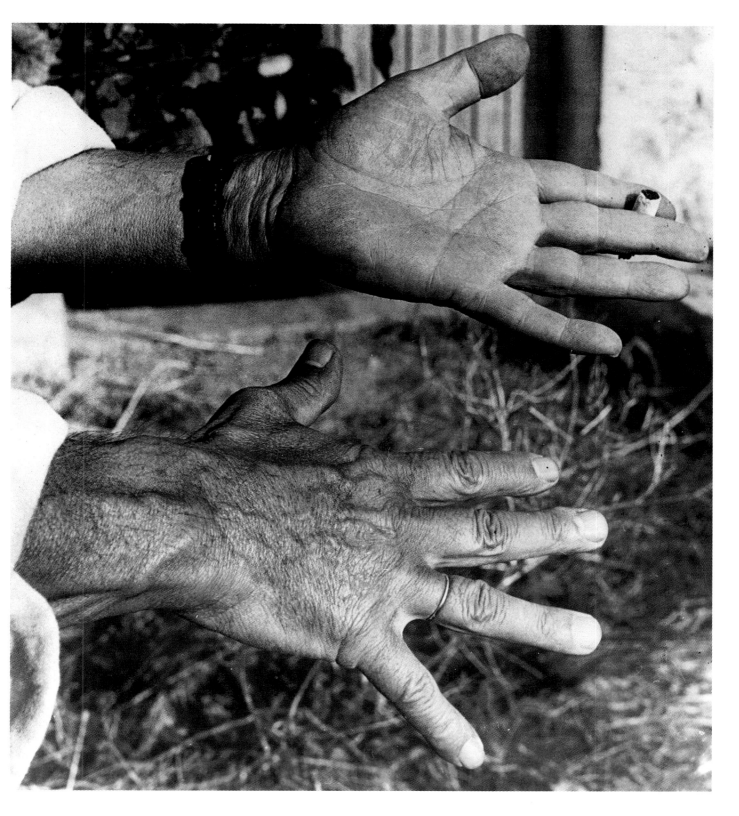

Starting in 1920, Picasso summered regularly on the Riviera, wandering between Cannes, Monte Carlo, Cap d'Antibes, and Juan-les-Pins, first with his wife Olga and their son Paulo, then with his mother or Marie-Thérèse Walter and their daughter Maya in the thirties and, in 1939, with the photographer Dora Maar, his companion at that time. Picasso had already discovered Grimaldi Castle in 1923. According to Dor de la Souchère, "one day as he was passing by a deserted building in Antibes, he surprised a group of children sneaking through a hole into the sun-drenched ruin. He bent down and followed! And that's how Picasso first burst onto the scene of this mysterious fortified castle."

Some years later, when the painter was staying on the Boulevard Albert Ier in 1939, he pointed the site out to his secretary Sabartès from the terrace of his apartment: "Those towers are part of Grimaldi Castle. Someone once offered to sell it to me for twenty thousand francs. It's a museum now. Farther off you can see the Fort-Carré. We'll go and swim at the beach behind it. Just wait till you see the pebbles! If it weren't for the haze, you could see Nice from here. I'll take you there."

In August of 1939, Picasso painted *Fishing by Lamplight in Antibes,* one of his largest pictures, with the canvas hanging flat against the wall; today in the New York Museum of Modern Art, the painting came back to Antibes for the summer of 1981, one hundred years after the artist's birth. The painter spent the war years in Paris, where he joined the Communist Party. Accompanied by his new companion, the painter Françoise Gilot, who was just a third as old as he when they met in 1943, Picasso again returned to Grimaldi Castle in 1945, for an exhibition of children's drawings organized by the British Council.

After accepting Dor de la Souchère's invitation and moving with Françoise Gilot to Golfe-Juan, where he stayed in the house of the engraver Louis Fort, Picasso — in love and overjoyed to be back on the Mediterranean — was particularly struck by the powerful heritage of antiquity on the Museum's terrace, which had once been the Acropolis of Antipolis.

Inspired by Mythology, he decided to paint frescoes on the third floor of the castle, using a light range of sky and sand colors that breaks totally with the grey and brown tones he had used in Paris during the war.

"Do you see that old tower and the terrace overlooking the sea? I worked like a maniac there," Picasso later told Brassaï. "I didn't have any of the supplies you need to make frescoes... It's too risky to paint right onto the wall... They bought me some execrable sackcloth and gave me some old canvases and plywood... But I finally settled on big sheets of fibrocement and painted some frescoes for them... I'm going to leave everything in a room there; they want to turn the place into a Picasso Museum. I might give them some other stuff I made while I was there, some bone and stone carvings" (Brassaï, *Conversations avec Picasso*).

"I did my best in Antibes, and it was a pleasure because, at least that once, I knew I was really working for the people."

From August to December, according to Dor de la Souchère, Picasso worked "like mad" on the third floor of the Museum. Since he wanted to paint even at night, he had reflectors installed. Lacking material, he ordered vellum paper and brushes in Paris. "In the meantime," Françoise Gilot recalls, "he went down to the port with Sima and stocked up on boat paint because he thought it would hold up better in the local climate. As this paint is usually used on wood, he decided to paint on plywood and sheets of fibrocement. He bought the same brushes house painters use and set to work the next day, as soon as everything had been delivered" (Françoise Gilot, *Vivre avec Picasso*).

The originality of the Antibes Picassos lies in their mythological inspiration, the use of new materials, and the fact that the works are now dislayed in the actual setting where they were created.

Dor de la Souchère and Picasso in front of *Triptych*, Antibes, 1948. Photo: Denise Colomb.

Towards the end of his stay, short on material, Picasso did not hesitate to take several old canvases, which seemed worthless enough to him, from the Museum storeroom and paint over them, as the Museum staff, working with the Research Laboratory of the Museums of France, has recently shown (*A Travers Picasso*, catalogue n° 4). Thus, *The Sea Urchin Eater* was painted over the *Portrait of General Vandenberg*, a World War I hero and founding member of the Friends of the Antibes Museum. Similarly, *Still Life with Black Shut-*

Françoise Gilot, Picasso and his nephew Javier Vilato on the Golfe-Juan beach, 1948. Photo: Robert Capa, Magnum.

Picasso and Françoise Gilot in the studio with *La Joie de Vivre*, 1946. Photo: Michel Sima.

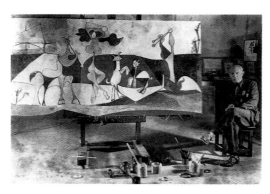

ters hides the *Portrait of a Girl* painted by Caroline Commanville, Flaubert's niece and heir, who spent the last years of her life in Antibes. The Curator later evoked these "appropriations" with humor: "One day, for a hypothetical inventory, I was looking through the storeroom for a terrible portrait of yet another Antibes army officer, leaning on his sword as if it were some kind of a crutch. Unable to locate it, I mentioned my disappointment to Picasso: he just grinned! Lacking canvas, he had scraped off the portrait and replaced it with one of the Museum's masterpieces, *The Sea Urchin Eater...* The Grimaldi Museum possessed nothing but daubs, beaming portraits of the officers who liv-

ed in this army town. One day Picasso came in; his piercing eyes looked around the room in appraisal. Finally, he quipped, 'Move over and make a little room for the young!' I knew exactly what he meant."

The painter divided his time between the beach in the morning and the Grimaldi Museum in the afternoon and evening, working on several pictures at once. As he worked, various friends and acquaintances would stop in to visit: Eluard and his wife Nush, Marcel Cachin, Hemingway, Cocteau, Sabartès, Léger, Aragon, Matisse, and Prévert, who recalled that once, as they contemplated the setting sun, Picasso remarked: "Nobody has ever painted that, but we'll have to try one of these days."

Three principal themes nurtured Picasso's work in Antibes: first, mythology, nymphs, fauns, centaurs, and sirens; second, nature, as can be seen in works reflecting the Antibes environment — so well evoked by the title of a limited edition that later reproduced a good part of it, *Faunes et Flore d'Antibes* (Le Pont des Arts, 1960) — and the Mediterranean fishermen, fish, and sea urchins, as well as the painted and sculpted variations on the two emblematic animals of Antipolis, the goat and the owl; finally, the nude, found in large compositions where the Cubist heritage can be seen in the geometrical simplification of the female body, several parts

of which are "listed" simultaneously in a completely unrealistic way.

Done on sheets of plywood and fibro-cement in thirteen colors of oil-based paint — which have not faded in forty years — the works sometimes include pencil and charcoal. The charcoal — e.g., in the arc lights — was brought to the artist by a filmmaker friend working in the Victorine studios in Nice. There may have been shortages after the war, but Picasso always managed to come up with supplies and adapt them to

Picasso painting a still life on the studio floor, 1946.
Photo: Michel Sima.

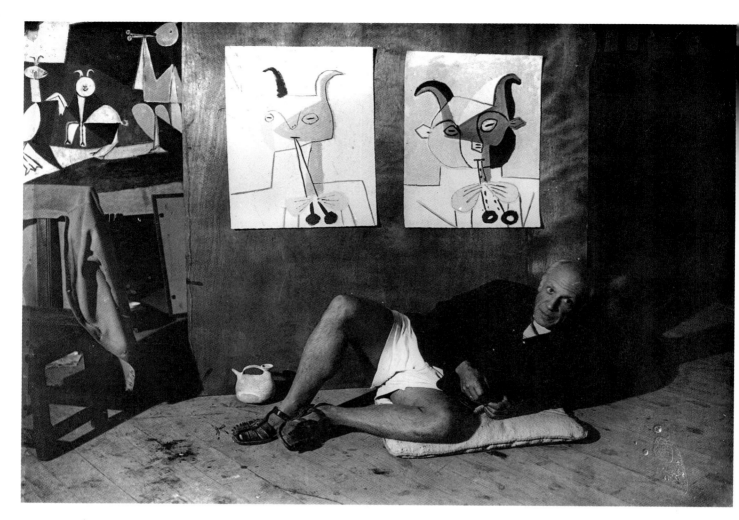

Picasso on a cushion in front of two fauns next to *La Joie de vivre* (first state), 1946. Photo: Michel Sima.

the special requirements of the castle. In the still lifes, Picasso did some quite innovative experiments, trying, for example, to dissociate drawing from color, which he placed next to the outline and sometimes outside of the form like a flat, colored shadow (*Still Life with Guitar*). He painted *The Keys to Antibes* directly onto the wall of his third-floor studio; another nude was painted on glass, and the film Paul Hasaerts made in 1948 shows how it was created with just a few strokes of white.

The photographs taken by Sima, who stopped by the studio every evening, show the successive stages in the paintings. Thus, in *La Joie de Vivre,* we see how Vauban's ramparts were replaced by a clear sky, the heads of the figures reduced in size to emphasize their monumentality, the range of colors simplified, and the curvaceous central nymph opposed to her more static two companions. Similarly, in the *Triptych with Centaur,* the infrared camera used by a research team revealed how the

14

different "anatomical" drawings of the figures finally gave way to a drawing so simple and pure that it cannot but remind one of the cave paintings at Lascaux.

Between August 31 and October 28, the artist did forty-five works on paper in preparation for the large paintings. Eleven studies in oil and India ink represent fauns and centaurs. Sixteen mythological drawings in graphite, sometimes highlighted in red chalk, develop a theme the artist had first started exploring in Ménerbes in July, 1946. Twelve studies for a female nude, done in three days (November 9-11), are in the spirit of the large nudes and show sculptural figures set on large bases. Three studies in grisaille (charcoal and oil) for the *Triptych* and three still lifes with sea urchins elaborate variations on the spiral, which is found, like an emblem, in numerous drawings. Finally, two paintings, recently located and purchased by the town of Antibes, are now back in the museum where they were born.

The source of these bacchanalian Antibes women can be found in a fairly accurate copy of Poussin's *Triumph of Pan* (Louvre Museum) that Picasso did in his studio on the Rue des Grands Augustins during the war. It was the first time he showed an interest in the satyrs and nymphs that were to provide the rich theme he incessantly modified and expanded in the Antipolis Series.

Picasso's studio on the third floor of the Museum. In the background, the fresco sketched on the wall, 1946. Photo: Michel Sima.

Françoise Gilot, Vallauris, 1947. Photo: Willy Maywald.

The Works in the Picasso Donation

"A Picasso is solid *and*
delicate. It is heavy *and* it
flies, like those big birds
of prey that hover
motionless in the air!
Picasso was, in a sense,
requisitioned by the
Antibes Museum. And we
redid the whole Castle to
display the works he did
there."

Dor de la Souchère

White Faun Playing a Double Flute,
1946. Oil-based paint and charcoal
on ochre vellum paper, 66 × 51 cm.

16

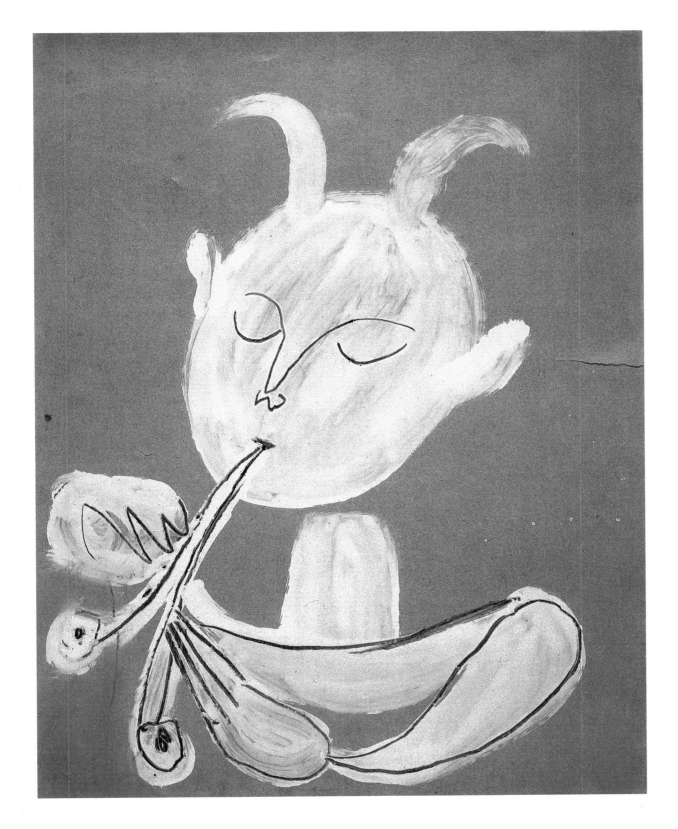

There are many sources that reveal the genesis and evolution of the works Picasso gave Antibes. First of all, the chronology of the works can be determined using Picasso's own indications, for he dated and numbered almost all of these works on the back. Then, Françoise Gilot's book *Vivre avec Picasso,* though it sometimes seems a bit like a settling of scores, is rich in information on how Picasso painted while they were living together in Antibes. Dor's diaries and writings on Picasso's stay are invaluable sources, as are the four hundred or so photographs that the sculptor Michel Sima took every evening during Picasso's stay in Antibes. Some of these were published in his book, prefaced by Sabartès, and illustrate poems by Eluard; others, carefully conserved in the Museum's archives, provide additional indications on the evolution of the works and the artist's way of painting. Sima's photographs also provide information on Picasso's lifestyle and how his studio, a large sunny room on the south side of the castle, was set up, with a matress for naps lying on the pink slab floor and a big table with dishes for lunches next to another table covered with cans and brushes. They also show an owl in a cage — the very one found in various paintings and drawings — set on the floor between two easels, and the artist's many friends — from Eluard to Cocteau, and Matisse to Hemingway and Sabartès — who came to visit him while he was working in Antibes.

In addition to these historical sources, scientific study of the Antibes paintings done in 1983 by a team from the Research Laboratory of the Museums of France produced more than a few surprises. Microscopic samples, x-rays of the pictures, and over one hundred and sixty photographs taken with different lighting reveal the genesis of the works and the transformations Picasso brought to these compositions, on which he sometimes worked simultaneously.

Forty years after Picasso's stay in Antibes, these diverse sources enable museum visitors to piece together the story of how the artist lived and worked there.

The Antibes Picassos — created in 1946 in Grimaldi Castle, which they have never left — changed the destiny, and name, of the Museum. They occupy a very special place in the artist's work. When he did them, Picasso was sixty-five, in love, soon to be a father again, and at the height of his creative powers. After the austere compositions of the wartime period, which Picasso spent in his Paris studio on the Rue des Grands-Augustins, surrounded by grey still lifes with empty pans, sparse compositions of fishbones and skulls, and tragic portraits of the *Crying Woman* (where Dora Maar is a shrill figure painted in strident shades of bright green, purple,

scarlet red, and lemon yellow), the Antibes works were invaded by a sunny palette of sand and sea colors combined with moss green and ochre shades: the Cubist palette wed the colors of the Mediterranean in a Dionysian return to nature.

But it is the *Flower-Woman,* the dancing woman, twenty-year-old Françoise Gilot whose presence is most strongly felt in these new paintings, from which all violent contrasts have disappeared. Apart from several accents for the coral of the sea urchins, there are no reds, but rather a very soft pink — rarely seen since early

in the century — which is sometimes used to enrich these compositions.

Some of them are highly simplified, monumental decorative panels, which Picasso felt a strong urge to do after the small formats of the war years. One of his reasons for coming to the Grimaldi Museum was to do murals on its walls; these works are based on linear black drawings on white grounds and, in this, resemble the work his friend Matisse was doing at the Chapel of Vence at about the same time.

One of the most novel things about these works is the artist's reduced pal-

Left: *Yellow and Blue Faun Playing a Double Flute,* 1946. Oil, oil-based paint, and charcoal on vellum paper, 66 × 51 cm.

Right: *Grey Faun's Head,* 1946. Oil and pencil on vellum paper, 66 × 51 cm.

Centaur and Ship, October 19, 1946.
Oil and oil-based paint on paper,
50 × 65 cm. Located and purchased
in 1985.

Picasso in front of a study for *La Joie de Vivre, Centaur and Ship*, 1946.
Photo: Michel Sima.
This photograph allowed the work
to be located.

ette: the twenty-four pictures and fourteen works on paper are all done in the same thirteen colors, pigment mixtures used for the most part on large surfaces and applied in large blocks; the colors show no modulation whatever, and cover the grounds of the compositions. Interestingly, the photographs of the studio show neither tubes nor a palette, but cans of paint; and various eye-witnesses (Françoise Gilot, Michel Sima, Dor de la Souchère) all confirm the recent tests done by the Laboratory of the Museums of France. Picasso was, in fact, using boat paint that he bought by the can, and applying it with flat medium paintbrushes instead of the traditional art brushes. This runny paint often led him to work on the floor, as the photographs also show.

The artist sometimes drew directly in the wet paint with charcoal or pencil, covering the surface with blackened furrows. The supports chosen by the artist were also utterly original: he used water-resistant plywood for the still lifes with sea urchins and the portraits, and prefabricated sheets of fibrocement (asbestos, 120 × 250 cm), for the horizontal triptych *Ulysses,* the vertical Centaur triptych and the single panels *Still Life with Ewer, Nude in a White Bed,* and *La Joie de Vivre.* The artist had two reasons for his highly unusual choices. The first was necessity: because of shortages during the postwar years, canvas, stretchers,

and tacks were very hard to come by. The correspondence (published in the *Revue de l'Art,* nº 12, 1971) between Matisse in Nice, Camoin in Saint-Tropez, and Bonnard in Cannes shows how hard it was for the three friends to procure linen after the war. What a windfall when there were old bedsheets to cut up! Artists were careful to save the tacks when they changed stretchers, as well as their empty tubes of paint, as metal was quite scarce at the time.

The second reason for Picasso's unusual choices was the climate. Perched like a figurehead above the sea, the humid Museum can be absolutely torrid in the summer heat, but is freezing cold when the winter winds arrive. Picasso wanted to be sure his supports would resist the hard climate, and thus settled on the kind of wood used to build fishing boats and the fibrocement used to construct houses around Antibes.

Picasso and *La Joie de Vivre,* 1946.
Photo: Michel Sima.
The first state of the composition shows the ramparts that Vauban built around the castle.

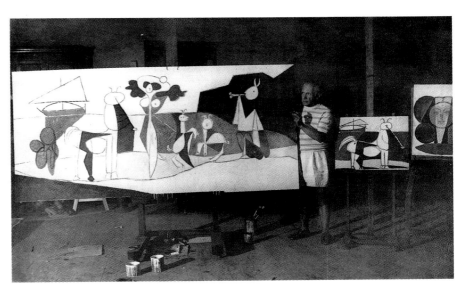

"Every time I come to Antibes, I am struck anew by a feeling of antiquity. Before, I had done centaurs and satyrs; in Ménerbes, I did a lot of them, but I hadn't been to Antibes for years... Artistic creation is a matter of time, place, and circumstance. Anything and everything can be a point of departure. You take a swallow, and it hits you."
Picasso to Dor de la Souchère, 1956.

La Joie de Vivre or *Antipolis*, 1946.
Oil and oil-based paint on
fibrocement, 120 × 250 cm.
In the final version, the sky fills the
entire background of the
composition. The heads of the
figures have been reduced in size;
and this makes them look
monumental.

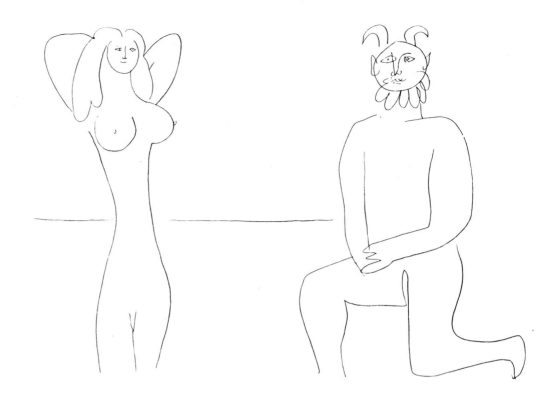

*Standing Nymph and Kneeling Faun
in Profile*, 1946. Graphite on vellum
paper, 51 × 66 cm.

*Seated Faun in Profile Playing a
Double Flute, Seated Nymph with
Tambourine, Large Standing Goat*,
1946. Graphite on vellum paper,
51 × 66 cm.

"Of all the characters in Classical mythology, it would seem that Picasso is most drawn to those who embody permanent metamorphosis: the Minotaur, the Centaurs, the Fauns. And he is himself in a never-ending state of metamorphosis. He has never got locked into one style, and has always transformed everything in his reach or field of vision... Whether transforming something directly or recording his characters' experiences and changes, he has always refused to accept that any being or object could be permanent or unchanging."
Michel Leiris, *Picasso et la Comédie Humaine*, Verve, 1954.

Seated Faun in Profile Playing a Double Flute, Dancing Nymph with Tambourine, Bearded Centaur with Trident, 1946. Graphite on vellum paper, 55 × 66 cm.

Standing Faun Playing a Double Flute, Seated Nymph with Tambourine and Dish of Fruit, and Bearded Centaur with Trident, 1946. Graphite on vellum paper, 51 × 66 cm.

Faun's Head in Grisaille with Three Figures in the Margins, 1946. White oil-based paint and charcoal on bistre paper, 43.5 × 47.5 cm.

Faun's Head in Grisaille, 1946. White oil-based paint and charcoal on wrapping paper, 50 × 56 cm.

Centaur with Trident and Two Fauns' Heads, 1946. White oil-based paint and charcoal on bistre paper, 48.5 × 43.5 cm.

The industrial paint he used to cover these supports was just as logical a choice. He had come to paint the castle's walls, but was forced to abandon this project after the Three Geometrical Faces of *The Keys to Antibes,* due to the humidity of the Museum's walls. Today one can only admire the logic behind Picasso's choice of materials, and how intelligently and economically he adapted them to the setting. In keeping with this logic, the artist wisely stipulated, at the time of the donation, that his works never be loaned to other museums; they have thus never left the Museum and are perfectly conserved. "They will stay in Antibes," Picasso once remarked, "and anyone who wants to see them will have to go there."

The sculptor Michel Sima, a student of Zadzine's, had been introduced to Picasso by the poet Robert Desnos. Deported during World War II, when he came back he stayed at his friend Dor's in Cannes. Hoping to turn the Museum into a haven for artists, Dor suggested to Sima that he come and work in the Museum. After getting back in touch with Picasso, Sima brought him to the castle and introduced Dor to him. The Museum had been closed since 1939. Reminders of the last Napoleon exhibition could still be seen on the second floor: military uniforms, firearms, posters and Imperial orders that had been exhibited in *Return from Elba* (1937). The

The Goat. 1946. Oil and pencil on plywood, 120 × 150 cm.

The magical world of childhood that was so familiar to Picasso — who always saw things in a totally new and fresh way — guided him in his treatment of every subject. He was also perfectly familiar with the many changes and transformations that make up the history of art. But, as he reinvented the forms of art, he discovered brand new forms that express his own emotions and owe nothing to the past. "I don't seek," he was fond of saying. "I find."

Triptych, Satyr, Faun, and Centaur with Trident, 1946. Oil and charcoal on fibrocement, 248.5 × 360 cm.

walls were still covered with historical documents such as the petitions of the consuls of Antibes. The Room of Privileges (granted by Charles X to this Royalist town), the Room of Maps and Fortifications by Vauban, and the Aguillon Room, devoted to the restauration of the Roman aqueduct, were all covered over by a thick layer of dust that had been building up since the outbreak of World War II. On the third floor, reminders of a quarter century of archeological investigations were piled high: casts, amphoras, transcriptions, historical records, and boxes of items dating from the Museum's three art and history exhibitions, for which local artists and collectors had donated the objects, paintings, and family portraits that made up the Museum's "reserves."

Trying to find plaster to make a cast of the Greek "phallic stone" — the triple priapic homage that had so enchanted Picasso, now displayed next to *La Joie de Vivre* — the two friends went all the way to Cannes to a building supplies store, Lanteri, located on the Boulevard d'Alsace, and there discovered the nine sheets of fibrocement that were to become the *Triptych, Ulysses* (painted in 1947), *La Joie de Vivre, Large Nude,* and *Still Life with Ewer.*

The first painting, which Picasso spent several weeks on, was *La Joie de Vivre.* He called it that — using a title of Matisse's — because it was meant to symbolize the happiness he felt during his outings to the Golfe-Juan beach with Françoise Gilot and Sima. Picasso and Gilot had rented a small, rather uncomfortable — and, for that matter, rather ugly — house with flowered and striped wallpaper from the old Lacourière engraver Louis Fort; but they were happy there, and could swim undisturbed on the practically deserted nearby beach. Two children gamboling on the sand became the kids in *La Joie de Vivre;* the trio formed by Picasso, Sima, and Gilot was transformed into the Faun, Nymph, and Centaur. On the back of the painting, Picasso wrote *Antipolis* and dated the work 1946, signing with a faun's head.

When they went to the beach in Golfe-Juan — or to the beach at the foot of the Fort-Carré — they would look for interesting stones to carve. These carvings were first exhibited in 1981, at the Museum. Picasso's, grey and ovoid, were turned into fauns; Sima, on the other hand, carved pieces of glass that had been shaped and smoothed down by the sea. After bathing, they would stay at the beach and have lunch at Tétou's, or go to Marcel's in Golfe-Juan, or to the Bar de la Marine, and lunch with friends who happened to be in the area: Paul Eluard and Nush, Jacques Prévert (who would come over from Saint-Paul), Marcel Cachin, Ernest Hemingway, and, occasionally, American or

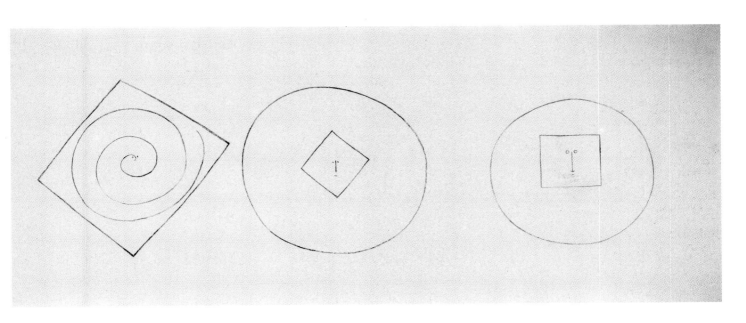

The Keys to Antibes, 1946. Graphite
on the wall of the third-floor studio
in the Museum, 106 × 253.5 cm.

Woman with Hairnet also known as *Woman with Green Hair*, 1949/1956. Original color lithograph, forth state, 66 × 50 cm.

Most of the works done during this period were inspired by Françoise Gilot.

French dealers (Pierre Loeb). It was on the beach in Golfe-Juan — cleaned everyday by a German prisoner — that they were nearly blown up by a German mine: one day as they were carrying back empty food cans they planned to use for mixing paint, Sima stopped Picasso from picking up a strange-looking plate just in the nick of time!

Compositionally, the large decorative panel *Triptych* could be said to stem from *La Joie de Vivre*. For this work, Picasso stood three sheets of fibrocement on end and placed one figure, amply drawn in black on a white ground, on each panel. The *Faun* and *Centaur* have changed places; the central nymph has been replaced by one of the two kids from *La Joie de Vivre*, shown gamboling between the other two figures.

The three studies painted in grisaille on bistre paper (dated October 16-17) show the rough shape of these figures and, already, the artist's desire to simplify. The *Centaur* took shape immediately, constructed on the perpendicular of the powerful chest and shoulders. The *Faun*, as shown by the three successive states photographed by Sima and the infrared shots taken by the Laboratory, began in a reclining position, and was later reduced in size, probably after the *Centaur* had been completed.

Dated October 31 and November 1, the sixteen studies for *La Joie de Vivre*, so freely drawn in graphite on vellum paper (placed horizontally), show the positioning of the main characters and minor figures (goats and kids) and the variations on their attributes (double flute, trident, tambourine, basket of fruit, fish, sea urchins). In the drawings, the figures are shown dancing in the curl of the wave. The decor exists only in the finished painting: on the right, the fortified ramparts of Antibes were replaced by a clear sky (however, the somber mass of the ramparts, which Sima photographed, can still be detected beneath the blue sky); on the left, a boat with a lateen sail behind the Centaur creates a second plane, which has also evolved. The entire pyramidal composition is centered around the dancer's tambourine, the only perfectly white note in the gradation of blues of the sky. The six vertical fauns painted in the same colors on paper, from August 31 to October 14, probably represent the intermediate stage between the studies drawn in graphite and the final painting, since a photograph of Sima's shows Picasso lying under two fauns, dated October 14, which closely resemble an intermediate state of *La Joie de Vivre*.

For *Grey Nude on a Green Ground,* the period photographs show only one change. A heavy volume painted in monochrome on a monochomatic ground, this work evokes Cézanne in the treatment of the body using cyl-

Head of a Woman with Chignon, 1953. Original black-and-white lithograph, pencil, 65 × 43 cm.

Still Life with Dish of Grapes, Guitar, and Two Apples on a Plate, 1946. Oil-based paint and charcoal on plywood, 95 × 175 cm.

"For better or worse, I have always used things according to the dictates of my passions. How sad for a painter who loves blondes to abstain from putting them in a picture just because they don't go with a basket of fruit! How abominable for a painter who hates apples to have to use them all the time just because they go so well with a tablecloth! Personally, I put everything I like into my pictures. Too bad for the things: they just have to get used to it."

Picasso, quoted by John Berger.

inder, sphere, and cone shapes. The twelve preparatory drawings in ink date from November 8 to November 12. The strange-looking figures closely resemble the Surrealistic filiform structures of the Dinard period, evoking certain mobiles that Calder was doing at that time. Drawn with a single line, the *Nudes* are reduced to ovoid masses balanced on geometric bases like fragile sculptures. Some of the sketches in the margins of these drawings concern other works: the triangular face of the *Nude in a White Bed,* the *Owl* in the *Still Life* of November 6, and (in the same drawing) a standing, hieratic *Nymph* that is close to the one in the large *Standing Nude* painted on glass.

The only work for which we do not have a preparatory drawing is, along with *Still Life with Watermelon,* the astonishing *Reclining Nude* painted on fibrocement, the stylization of which is as Cubistic as that of *Seated Nude.* But unlike the sculptural stillness of the latter, *Reclining Nude* is remarkable because of the simultaneous vision of the twisting body: the buttocks, stomach, and genitals, shown frontally, suggest that the figure is rolling over in bed, while another movement in the opposite direction begins in the spiral of the face, continues in the spiral of the arms, and ends in the triangle of the breasts, which are also represented both frontally and in profile. (According to Françoise Gilot, Ma-

These three studies for the painting show the stages in the geometrical elaboration of the forms. In the painting, drawing and color are juxtaposed, but not combined.

Still Life with Fruit, 1946. Oil-based paint and pencil on vellum paper, 66 × 51 cm.

Still Life with Dish of Grapes, 1946. Oil on paper. 50.5 × 65.5 cm.

Still Life with Three Lemons, Dish of Grapes, and Bottle, 1946. Oil-based paint and charcoal on vellum paper, 66 × 51 cm.

"When you start with a portrait and try, little by little, to pare it down to a pure form and essential volume, you cannot help but wind up with an egg. Similarly, if you start with an egg, and go in the opposite direction, you can end up with a portrait. But, in my opinion, this simplistic process of going from one extreme to the other has nothing to do with art. You must be able to stop in time."
Picasso, 1932.

Study of Owls, Faces, and Sea Urchins, November 7, 1946. Pencil on vellum paper, 51 × 66 cm. Notice the different versions of the face found in *Woman with Sea Urchins* (see page 45).

Right page: *Still Life with Owl and Three Sea Urchins*, 1946. Oil on plywood, 81.5 × 79 cm.

"Pablo loved to be surrounded by animals and birds. He was sometimes suspicious of his friends, but never of his pets. While he was still working at the Antibes Museum, Sima gave him a little owl he had found in the Museum's garden. One of its feet had been injured. We put a dressing on, and the wound slowly healed. He bought a cage and took it back to Paris, where he put it in the kitchen with his canaris, pigeons, and turtledoves."
Françoise Gilot, *Vivre avec Picasso.*

tisse was quite surprised by this Nude, and made several sketches of it, recently published by Pierre Schneider). The admirable thing about this series is its astonishing unity of inspiration and great stylistic diversity, made possible by a constant renewal of expressive possibilities. Prepared in a number of free, cursory, rapid and, one might say, stenographic drawings, Picasso stripped down his work more and more as the days went by, ridding it of anecdote and detail in favor of timeless and even classic themes.

Painted on wood, the two *Fishermen* were done on November 3, followed three days later by the *Woman with Sea Urchins* (the *Man Gulping Sea Urchins* was done about ten days later). Gilot describes the woman whom Picasso used as a model; and the successive stylizations of the face found in the vi-

Picasso and an owl with an injured foot, 1946. Photo: Michel Sima.

gnettes around the *owl* drawings dated November 7 again make it possible to follow the artist's train of thought. Very round in the first version, the woman was inscribed in the half-circle formed by the back of her chair, before being definitively flattened and stretched out laterally. Here again, Sima's photographs reveal the three states of the figure, and this is confirmed by Christian Lahanier's video study (*A travers Picasso,* catalogue n° 4).

In this group of works that are so singular in the artist's career, the eight paintings on canvas stand out as exceptions, in technique and size. The dimensions of these works are smaller, and their formats more traditional: four small still lifes may be considered Seascapes, while the larger *Man Gulping Sea Urchins* is a Figure. The light undercoatings reveal a surface that was scratched off before being painted over in zinc white (the undercoatings of the other paintings are whitewashed); and the edges of the canvases, under the tacks of the stretcher, show traces of several very different coats of paint. The backs of these canvases are very old. When we noticed these various features, we quickly realized that there was something quite odd about these canvases and decided to have them x-rayed. What we found was beyond our wildest expectations: *Man Gulping Sea Urchins, Still Life with Black Shutters,* and *Bouquet of Flowers*

Left page: *Seated Nude on a Green Ground*, 1946. Oil and oil-based paint on plywood, 165 × 174.5 cm.

Top: *Reclining Nude in a White Bed*, 1946. Oil on fibrocement, 120 × 250 cm.

Bottom: *Reclining Nude in a Blue Bed*, 1946. Oil, oil-based paint, and charcoal on plywood, 100 × 210 cm.

Seated Fisherman with Cap,
1946. Oil on plywood,
106.5 × 82 cm.

Left page: *Fisherman at a
Table,* 1946. Oil and oil-based
paint on plywood,
95.5 × 81 cm.

The x-ray of *Man Gulping Sea Urchins*, which reveals the portrait of General Vandenberg (1858-1977), an Antibes native and founding member of the Friends of the Museum.

Man Gulping Sea Urchins, 1946. Oil and charcoal on a re-used canvas (*Portrait of General Vandenberg*), 130.5 × 81 cm.

"When he got to the studio that evening, Picasso took the only canvas he had and started painting a basket, sea urchins, a piece of bread, a knife, and a wine bottle with a glass turned upside down over it. Afterwards, he painted more sea urchins in another way, using them to complement other subjects; and, a little later, on the day of my departure, he began to prepare a canvas whose dimensions seemed right to him for the *Man Gulping Sea Urchins*. I remember asking Picasso why he was so interested in sea urchins. 'I'm not,' he answered. 'I'm neither interested nor uninterested in them. They're like everything else. It's not my fault if I saw them. If I had been thinking about them already, I might not have so much as noticed them, even if they had been right in front of me. Our eyes like to be surprised. If you *want* to see something, you'll be distracted by the idea of seeing it.'"
Jaime Sabartès.

Woman with Sea Urchins, 1946. Oil on plywood, 119 × 83 cm.

"We had lunch almost everyday in Golfe-Juan at Marcel's. In front of the little café next door to the restaurant, there was a seafood (...) But it was October, and the only person the display really interested was the owner of the café. She was so fat, and her café so narrow, that she could barely fit inside. She couldn't have been more than a meter and a half tall, was as wide as she was high, and had the most farcical, craggy features (with a funny little turned-up nose) framed by little mahogany curls sticking out from under the bill of her hugh man's cap. While we were having lunch, we would often see her pacing back and forth outside with a basket of sea urchins in one hand and a sharp pointed knife in the other, on the look-out for potential customers. (...) The *Woman Eating Sea Urchins* was begun in a realistic style. Everything in the portrait was recognizable: the turned-up nose, the curls, the cap, and the big dirty apron. But once he had finished the drawing, Pablo went back and deleted a new detail every day, until nothing was left but a simplified, almost vertical form — and the plate of sea urchins to recall the original inspiration."
Françoise Gilot, *Vivre avec Picasso*.

Woman with Sea Urchins, 1946, first state.

*Still Life with Lime, Two Fish, and
Two Moray Eels*, 1946. Oil, pencil,
and charcoal on vellum paper,
66 × 51 cm.

*Still Life with Lime, Two Fish, and
Moray Eel on a Grey Ground*, 1946.
Oil and charcoal on canvas,
38 × 55 cm.

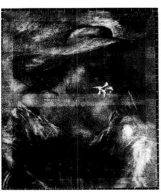

Still Life with Black Shutters, Lemon, Moray Eel, Mullets, Cuttlefish, and Three Sea Urchins, 1946. Oil on re-used canvas (*Girl with Wide-Brimmed Hat*, painted by Caroline Commanville, Flaubert's niece),
60.5 × 73.5 cm.

Ulysses and the Sirens, 1947. Oil
and oil-based paint on three sheets
of fibrocement, 360 × 250 cm.

In both the large compositions and
the small drawings, Picasso "lists"
forms, which have been reduced to
simple, metaphoric signs (e.g., Ulysses' boat and the fish).

were painted over older pictures that had been painted by someone else. Picasso sometimes began by coating the older painting over in white (the two *Still Lifes with Limes, Man Gulping Sea Urchins, Still Life with Black Shutters*). At other times, he simply turned the canvas around and worked "backwards" (*Still Life with Two Cuttlefish and Two Octopuses*), or glued on a sheet of paper and used the stretched canvas for its elasticity, as in the case of *Vase of Foliage,* on the back of which one can still make out the original signature of Carlos Reymond, who had participated in the Museum's first exhibition of modern art in 1928. His *Little Bridge,* which can be made out on the x-ray, was n° 114 in the first catalogue that Dor edited for the Museum.

Short on material, Picasso had simply taken some canvases from the Museum's reserves (if the accumulation of daubs in the attic can be called that). Thirty-six years after Picasso painted over these canvases, our x-rays spectacularly revealed the *Portrait of General Vandenberg* under the *Man Gulping Sea Urchins,* and a *Girl with Wide-Brimmed Hat* behind the *Still Life with Black Shutters.*

The history of art is full of repainted canvases: the Pope's "trouser makers" clothed the angels and, when virtue came back into fashion, covered the breasts that had delighted generations of less prudish eyes. Painters themselves have sometimes, usually after a lapse of several years, reworked or completely repainted their own canvases. But cases of one artist covering over, transforming, or destroying another artist's work are far less frequent.

Picasso (here too a precursor ?) offered himself an incestuous treat. The charming *Girl with Wide-Brimmed Hat* is today safely resting behind black blinds, with a sea urchin in her mouth and a moray eel around her neck! The barefoot fismerman greedily gulping down a sea urchin is none other than General Vandenberg, the World War I hero who had commanded the Algerian Zouaves (at about the time of Picasso's birth) and ended his career in 1925 as a Commander in the Legion of Honor and Governor of Libya. After retiring to his home town, the General became one of the five founding members of the Society of Friends of the Museum, the group whose fundraising efforts allowed the town of Antibes to purchase Grimaldi Castle. That year, Picasso was swimming in Juan-les-Pins with a beautiful girl of seventeen, Marie-Thérèse Walter.

The Ceramics, Sculptures, Engravings, and Tapestries

"An emblematic animal, the bull, is found in Picasso's work from his childhood up to his death. It often represents the artist himself and is a dual symbol of Spain and Mediterranean antiquity, the keys to the artist's inspiration."

Standing Bull, Vallauris, 1949. Ceramic sculpture with painted décor; masked head and horns attached; 30 × 40 × 30 cm. Photo: Marianne Greenwood.

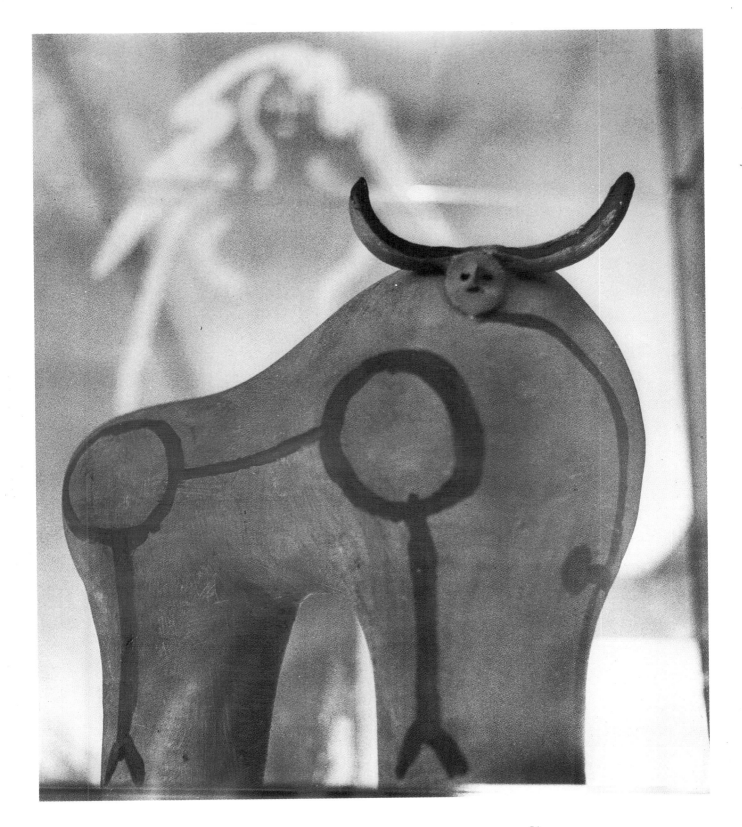

The Ceramics

Tanagra with Amphora, Vallauris, 1949. Wheeled and modeled figurine, 45 × 33 × 11 cm.

In 1948, Picasso gave the Museum seventy-seven ceramic dishes, vases, statuettes, and animals he had made during the two summers following his stay in Antibes, which he spent with his family (Françoise and their two children, Claude and Paloma) in Vallauris, at a villa called La Galloise. He was very interested in ceramics, which he had discovered while experimenting one summer in Georges Ramie's studio. Picasso was fascinated by this medium that combines painting and sculpture, the mysteries of the kiln and docile suppleness of fresh clay. "I spend my days learning to paint," he wrote Marie-Thérèse Walter in June 1948. "I think I've even made a little progress. I'm working on painted sculptures." The idea of working for a large public and embodying his visual universe in everyday objects may partly explain Picasso's enthusiasm in this studio, where he worked right alongside the craftsmen, who were quite stimulated by his energy. But his inventive imagination quickly pushed all other concerns aside. From October 1947 to October 1948, he turned out nearly two thousand pieces, radically renewing the potter's traditional art. His whimsical transformations of the clay gave birth to owls, doves, and "tanagras." A handle was turned into a wing or a horn; a press of the thumb into the fresh clay, and a vase became a kneeling tanagra or a condor's head. With just a few brushstrokes, he could enhance a wing, a dress pleat, or the curve of a breast or an arm.

Picasso would sometimes take pieces of broken Provençal pottery and amuse himself by decorating these clay fragments with elements inspired by the black figures of antiquity, thus totally changing the original.

"Picasso saw a jug as a woman with her arms folded behind her head; an owl quite naturally became a vase; and nothing more resembled a tall, rangy woman with her arms against her body than a long-necked vase... Nothing could resist Pablo's eyes and hands; he quickly became the center of attention and soul of the workshop; the craftsmen all worked for and through Picasso, who was always absorbed and fascinated by whatever piece he was modeling, or shaping on the potter's wheel, and always eager to see the latest works emerge from the kiln" (Pierre Cabanne, Le Siècle de Picasso).

Fifty-five of these works were exhibited at the Maison de la Pensée Française in Paris in 1949.

Picasso was particularly intrigued by the potter's "blind palette," which the kiln reveals and transforms: his use of incisions, enamelling, glazes, and firing in the Antibes dishes (still lifes, female faces, fauns) and pitchers (frequently decorated with nudes) shows how greatly his ability to learn depended on his ability to disobey the rules. The largest pieces are truly animal sculptures, one of the favorite themes of the artist who so loved to surround himself with animals.

Dish Decorated with Faun's Head Motif, Vallauris, 1947, 32 × 38 cm.

Dish Decorated with Smiling Face, Vallauris, 1948, 32 × 38 cm.

54

Oval dishes with painted décors, Vallauris. The ceramics done during the first year at Vallauris are, for the most part, paintings on dishes that the potters had prepared for Picasso.

Dish with Eggplant, Vallauris, 1949, 32 × 38 cm.

Dish with Eggs and Sausage, Vallauris, 1949, 32 × 38 cm.

"Art is never chaste; it should be forbidden to innocent ignoramuses. People who have not been sufficiently prepared should never be brought into contact with it. Yes, art is dangerous. If it's chaste, it isn't art."
Picasso, quoted by Antonina Vallentin.

The Sculptor Resting, 1933. Etching, 19.3 × 26.7 cm. Gift of the Friends of the Museum, 1986.

Right page: *Woman's Head with Chignon*, Boisgeloup, 1932. Original cement sculpture, 128.5 × 54.5 × 62.5 cm. Gift of the artist, 1950.

Left: *Seated Nude with Painter and Sculpted Head*, 1933. Etching, 26.8 × 19.4 cm.

Right: *Young Sculptor at Work*, 1933. Etching, 26.7 × 19.4 cm.

The Antibes Museum's new vocation led Picasso, in the period following his stay in Antibes, to make more major gifts. In 1950, he gave the Museum two of his monumental cement sculptures, the *Women's Heads* (1931-1932), which belong to the series of works realized in the early thirties at the Château de Boisgeloup, located near the town of Gisors in the Eure region. When he moved to the château, Picasso had not sculpted for some fifteen years. But, tempted by the spacious stables facing the main buildings on his newly acquired estate, he secretly realized a series of sculptures inspired by the perfect profile of Marie-Thérèse Walter, whom he had met three years earlier. "I was just seventeen," she later recalled. "I was an innocent kid and knew nothing about life or Picasso. Absolutely nothing! One day I went to do some shopping at the Galeries Lafayette, and Picasso saw me coming out of the subway. He simply grabbed me by the arm and announced: 'I'm Picasso. You and I are going to do great things together.'" For Picasso, this young girl, whom the painter's biographers and friends unanimously agree was a delightful incarnation of carefree youth, represented a happy contrast with his painful married life and increasingly frequent fights with Olga.

"She became the radiant dream of youth — in the background, but always in reach — that nurtured his work. She was interested in nothing but sports and never did enter Pablo's intellectual life... Yet she haunted his existence in a very poetic way, as was painfully obvious whenever she was not around, for Picasso could not stand to be separated from her," Françoise Gilot writes. "She had the purest of Grecian profiles; the whole series of portraits Pablo painted between 1927 and 1935 resembled her quite exactly." In his paintings, as in the 1933 *Sculptor's Studio* engravings for Vollard (which, significantly, represent the artist at work in a staging articulated around Classical references), the same woman's face is found, but reconstructed beyond the limits of strict retinal resemblance. Brassaï, who photographed the Boisgeloup statues for

The Parable of the Sculptor

"She was a tall, very blond girl with a fair complexion and refreshing laugh. Picasso met her in the street and was as taken by her youth, sculptural body, and blond hair as by her vivacious, easy-going temperament and calm, cheerful character, so impervious to mental torment. Marie-Thérèse Walter was carefree enough not to worry about what the future of their relationship would be and realistic enough to be satisfied with the time a married man could find for her. She knew how sensitive Olga was and always stayed in the background, but her presence triumphantly invaded Picasso's work in a way that leaves no doubt about her place in the artist's life."
Antonina Vallentin.

Left page: the two monumental *Woman's Heads*, donated by Picasso in 1950, as photographed by Brassaï in 1931 at Boisgeloup. Behind: *Head of Woman with Chignon*.

Woman's Head with Big Eyes in the studio at the Château de Boisgeloup, 1931. Photo: Brassaï.

Marie-Thérèse, the Boisgeloup model, with her daughter Maya in 1933. Photo: Pablo Picasso.

The sculpture studio in the stables at Boisgeloup, 1933. Photo: Brassaï.

Right page: Picasso at the Grimaldi Museum, 1948.
Photo: Denise Colomb.

tographed the Boisgeloup statues for an issue of André Breton's new review *Minotaure,* later gave a striking account of seeing the statues for the first time: "Oddly enough, in spite of a natural penchant, Picasso had not sculpted anything since the 1914 absinth glasses. He only took up sculpting again in 1929, and in the utmost secrecy. When I went to visit him, he brought me out to the stables and opened up one of the large stalls: we were literally blinded by the whiteness of a whole tribe of sculptures... What surprised me most was the curving fullness of the forms. The explanation was that a new woman had come into Picasso's life: Marie-Thérèse. He had met her by chance, on the Rue La Boétie, and had painted her for the first time just a year earlier, on December 16, 1931, in *The Red Armchair.* He had been taken by her youth, her cheerful laugh, and her liveliness. He loved the blondness of her hair, her radiant complexion, and her statuesque body... The day he met her, his paintings began to undulate... At no other point in his career were his paintings so undulating, all sinuously curving intertwined arms and wavy hair... Most of the statues I saw in the stables bore the mark of this 'new look,' which was so striking in the large bust of Marie-Thérèse leaning forward: the head is almost Classical, due to the flat forehead that joins the straight nose with no break, to form a line that was invading all of Picasso's work. In the *Sculptor's Studio* series that Picasso was then engraving for Vollard, monumental, almost spherical heads were also present in the background. They were not just figments of his imagination! How surprised I was to see them in skin and bone, or rather sculpted in the round, all curves, with increasingly prominent noses and bulging eyes: they looked like some barbarian goddess" (Brassaï, *Conversations avec Picasso*).

The Engravings

Paloma and Her Doll on a Black Ground, 1952. Original black-and-white lithograph, 70 × 55 cm.

Picasso, Françoise and their children, Claude et Paloma, moved to Vallauris.

Dove on a Black Ground, Vallauris, 1949. Black-and-white lithograph, 60 × 73 cm.

Many of the Musem's engravings are based on the same themes — portraits, still lifes, animals, Bacchanalia, and even sea urchins! — as the paintings and drawings. Others show typical scenes from Picasso's world, such as families of acrobats, bullfights, and images from the last years of his life. Engravings of a rare quality, done between 1933 and 1963, are on display in the intimacy of the Museum's smaller rooms, and allow visitors to appreciate the variety of techniques Picasso used: etching, aquatint, lithography, and, thanks to a recent gift, the linocut.

Picasso sometimes combined these techniques; but more importantly, as Bernhardt Geiser has pointed out, "he enriched them in an extraordinary way, discovering possibilities, operations, and resources that had never been noticed before him. This also applies to the field of lithography; and the boldness of his discoveries won the approval of the most experienced professionals."

With the help of the FRAM and the Friends of the Museum, the Museum has recently acquired seven of the Vollard engravings belonging to the *Sculptor's Studio* series, done at exactly the same time as the sculptures inspired by Marie-Thérèse Walter; they represent these sculptures on their bases, next to the bearded sculptor, who has a very Classical heroic look about him, and his model, in the sensual bloom of youth.

Bacchanalia with Black Bull,
Vallauris, 1959. Original color
linocut, 62 × 75 cm.

The works that Louise Leiris gave
the Museum are excellent examples
of the linocuts Picasso did at Vallauris. Picasso was often particularly innovative when exploring a new
technique, and the linocuts are no
exception. Most of these works are
based on the bull theme and were
used as posters for bullfights or the
annual pottery exhibitions of
friends.

The Tapestries

The Minotaur theme reappeared in Picasso's work in 1933 with the famous cover for André Breton's review of the same name. It was Breton who published the first pictures of Picasso's sculptures at the Château de Boisgeloup, photographed by Brassaï.
Following a commission from Amboise Vollard, his dealer, Picasso took the theme up again in a series that may be considered the high point of his work as an engraver, the *Minotauromachy*, conceived in Juan-les-Pins.
Picasso there portrayed himself as a powerful Bull-God, the dual symbol of Spain and Mediterranean Antiquity, which had become a powerful source of inspiration for the artist. The first Minotaur tapestry — one of the most valuable pieces in the Cuttoli Donation — was executed in 1935 by the Manufactures des Gobelins.

The Minotaur, drawing (first sketch for the collage on which the tapestry is based), 1928.

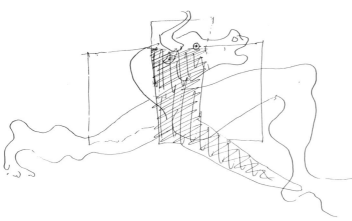

The Museum is indebted to Marie Cuttoli, a longtime friend of Picasso's, great collector, and patroness of the arts, for her tapestry donation. In 1953, Marie Cuttoli (1879-1973) gave the Museum a group of tapestries she had acquired from the Galerie Leiris; later, on several occasions, she purchased two tapestries of the same work, one for herself and one — as President of the Friends of the Museum — "for the Museum." From Shady Rock, her Cap d'Antibes villa, where Picasso often lunched with Dor, Georges Salles, Prévert, Eluard, and many others, she watched over the Museum and was always available to solve a problem or share her memories. J. Sabartès recalls that "Picasso had spent several days at Shady Rock; he came back from Ménerbes with all his luggage and the idea of staying there, on Madame Cuttoli's repeated entreaties." According to Sabartès, Marie Cuttoli confided in him: "He could have worked here at his leisure. You know my

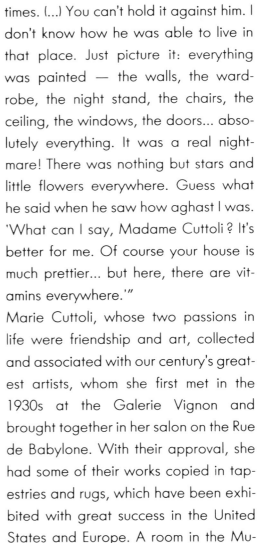

house. He would have had the sea at his disposal and all the peace and quiet anyone could desire, but... one day, he went off to Golfe-Juan. I don't know how he ever managed to work there. It was so tiny that he could hardly turn around; and in addition to being small and noisy, it was depressing. It was just the most uncomfortable place you can imagine. I went to see him a thousand times. (...) You can't hold it against him. I don't know how he was able to live in that place. Just picture it: everything was painted — the walls, the wardrobe, the night stand, the chairs, the ceiling, the windows, the doors... absolutely everything. It was a real nightmare! There was nothing but stars and little flowers everywhere. Guess what he said when he saw how aghast I was. 'What can I say, Madame Cuttoli? It's better for me. Of course your house is much prettier... but here, there are vitamins everywhere.'"

Marie Cuttoli, whose two passions in life were friendship and art, collected and associated with our century's greatest artists, whom she first met in the 1930s at the Galerie Vignon and brought together in her salon on the Rue de Babylone. With their approval, she had some of their works copied in tapestries and rugs, which have been exhibited with great success in the United States and Europe. A room in the Museum is named in her honor.

The Minotaur, 1935. Wool and silk,
Tapisserie des Gobelins,
142 × 237 cm.
Donated by Marie Cuttoli.

"If you marked all of the places I've
been on a map and linked the dots
with a line, the result might be a
Minotaur."
Picasso.

A Museum of Modern Art

"An arsenal of rose petals
on the pebbles of the
eagle's nest..."
Nicolas de Staël, 1954,
Antibes

Nicolas de Staël, *The Big Concert,*
1955. Oil on canvas, 350 × 600 cm.
Acquired in 1987. Photo: Lucarelli.

Top right: Nicolas de Staël, *Boats in Antibes*, 1955. Oil on canvas, 46 × 55 cm.

Top left: Nicolas de Staël, *Still Life with Candlestick on a Blue Ground*, 1955. Oil on canvas, 89 × 130 cm. Gift of Nicolas de Staël.

Bottom: Nicolas de Staël, *Le Fort-Carré*, 1955. Oil on canvas, 114 × 195 cm.

Nicolas de Staël has a particularly important place in the Museum, because of the presence there of his last canvases, and the role played by the town of Antibes in the artist's personal destiny...

In 1954, Nicolas de Staël rented a studio on the ramparts in Antibes, near the Museum, with a view of the sea and Fort Vauban. The Mediterranean had already attracted this Northerner, the son of a Baltic aristocrat and officer in the Czar's army. Starting in the 1950s, the light, colors, and landscapes of the Mediterranean exerted a real influence on him. "I sharpen my eyes on the Mediterranean sun," he once wrote.

Dor de la Souchère offered to organize an exhibition of de Staël's works in the third-floor studio that had been Picasso's. Over a six-month period, from September 1954 to March 1955, de Staël isolated himself and did three hundred and fifty-four paintings. His letters reveal his difficulties and alternating moods of enthusiasm and sudden discouragement (despite the visits of friends such as his confidant Jean Bauret, Douglas Cooper, Jacques Dubourg, and Pierre Lecuite). "Neither a prison nor a seaside haven, but somehow, inexplicably both," he said of the town where he arrived in autumn. "On the whole, Antibes is good for me."

Evolving from abstraction towards an attempted reconquest of the real, he worked in a liberty of expression that was so great as to be utterly vertiginous. "My goal is to renew myself continually, and it's not an easy thing to do. I know what lies under the violent surface of my paintings and their perpetual interplay of forces. It is something fragile, trying to approach goodness and the sublime... When I fling myself into a large canvas, and it turns out to be good, I always have the terrible feeling that chance played too big a part. It makes me dizzy, because it seems to me that the strength of the painting was created by accident, the wrong way, and that puts me into lamentable states of discouragement," he wrote in a letter in 1954. His balance was always fragile and always threatened. "I don't want to be systematically too far from my subject or too close to it; and I must have obsessions because without obsessions I wouldn't be able to do anything at all, but I don't know whether dream obsessions or direct obsessions are better, and it doesn't really matter, in the final

Nicolas de Staël in his studio on the Rue Gauguet in Paris, 1954. Photo: Denise Colomb.

analysis, as long as things find some kind of a balance, preferably an unbalanced balance." His production during this period was considerable. In the studio, he did nudes and very simple still lifes with bottles, casseroles, bread, and candlesticks. On his terrace, he painted seascapes in the strange white winter light and constructed views of the Fort-Carré behind vertical foregrounds of masts in the harbor.

As his painting was dematerialized by the use of such new tools as silk brushes and cotton wads, it was somehow purified. In October, a short trip to Spain,

"If the vertigo that I so value as an essential part of my being gently changed course to allow more concision and a greater, less harassing liberty, my days would be brighter."
"Pictorial space is a wall, but all of the birds in the world can fly freely there. At all depths."
Nicolas de Staël to Jean Dubourg, 1954.

"Staël painted. And when, of his own free will, he decided to take a hard-earned rest, he left us something unhoped-for, which has nothing to do with hope."
René Char.

which filled him with enthusiasm, allowed him to rediscover Velasquez, the "painter's painter" and "king of greys." In December, he went to see a Courbet exhibition in Lyon and was just as enthusiastic. Back in Antibes, "he produced a continuous stream of unique paintings with the sureness of a river flowing towards the sea — dense, radiant, richly resonant, and always sober works."

On March 5, his ascetic life was again interrupted by a short trip to Paris for the Domaine Musical's concert of pieces by Anton Webern. On the program, he noticed: "Violins: Red, Ochre/Red." Several days later, he began a large canvas (three meters by six) for his summer exhibition in Antibes: *The Big Concert.* On March 15, he tried to end his life "as a spiritual act, somehow harmless, in all goodness towards humanity." The next day, after leaving a letter for his family, he jumped to his death from the terrace of his studio. *The Big Concert* was left partly unfinished. Three months later, the Picasso Museum presented the first retrospective of the painter's work. On that particularly moving occasion, Françoise de Staël gave the Museum *Blue Still Life.*

Since 1981, the town of Antibes has acquired *Boats in Antibes, Le Fort-Carré* (with government funding), and the three preparatory drawings for these works. *The Big Concert,* which the artist's family had temporarily left in the

Top : Germaine Richier, *The Big Spiral*, 1956, on the terrace of the Museum, in front of three other bronzes by the same artist: *The Crazy Virgin*, 1946, *The Seed*, 1955, and *The Leaf*, 1948. Photo: Lucarelli.

Bottom: Germaine Richier, *Tomb of the Storm*, 1956. Stone, 162 × 42 × 32 cm. Photo: Lucarelli.

Germaine Richier, *The Leaf*, 1948. Bronze, 145 × 32 × 15 cm. Photo: Lucarelli.

Museum's keeping, on the wall where the artist had meant for it to hang, was purchased by the Museum in 1987, thanks to the generosity of private benefactors and funding from the French Ministry of Culture, the town of Antibes, and regional organisms. These works are now displayed as part of the Museum's permanent collections on the first floor; *The Big Concert* is on permanent display in Picasso's studio.

Germaine Richier is another artist to whom the Antibes Museum has devoted an important place. Seven works are on permanent display in the Sculpture and Fragrance Garden, including *Shadow of the Hurricane* and *Tomb of the Storm*, two of the artist's major stone sculptures, done in 1956. Donated by the artist at the time of her exhibition and by her family after her death, this group of sculptures was recently enlarged when the Museum purchased *The Big Spiral* (1956).

In the Days of the Child Septentrion

"There is a family feud
between Antibes Castle
and the Grimaldi Museum.
It was inevitable. When
the Museum moved into
the Castle, a precarious
balance was created —
and we must strive to
maintain that balance."
Dor de la Souchère, 1968.

Block embedded in the tower of the
castle. Epitaph of a woman, inscribed in accordance with the terms of a
will, 2nd century A.D.

74

Lapidary Collections

Though specialized in contemporary art since the Picasso Museum opened in 1948, Grimaldi Castle also houses an archeological collection, a reminder that the site was once a Roman *castrum* and that the museum founded in 1925 began as a museum of archeology and history made up essentially of funerary monuments and a small pottery collection.

Several large pieces and casts are now in the keeping of the archeological museum in Bastion Saint-André. The Musée Naval et Napoléonien and the Fondation Eilen-Roc present collections that remained in storage for many years at the Picasso Museum: archeological vestiges, arms, Napoleonic memorabilia, and nineteenth-century paintings.

The pieces that Dor kept on permanent display — including, of course, those that Picasso had chosen to be shown next to his own works — have been kept in the Picasso Museum.

As a complement to the major group of ceramics that Picasso gave the Museum in 1949, the Museum has kept a rare group of *large fountains* and *Biot earthenware jars* made in the eighteenth and nineteenth centuries (Poteries Auge-Laribe), which could be said to represent one stage in the long history of earthenware that spans from the amphoras of ancient times to Picasso's *Borage.*

1. Stela of the child Septentrion. Probable date: 2nd century A.D. 113 × 74 × 25 cm.
"To the Manes of the slave child Septentrion, aged twelve, who danced and entertained two days at the theatre in Antibes."

2. The Phallic Stone, 45.5 × 55.5 × 17 cm. Provenance unknown. The erotic inscription has been interpreted in diverse ways :
"Chime on, big villain, you too."
"May you be protected from the evil eye."
"May you be so lucky."

3. Raiela's stone. Funerary inscription, 3rd century   45.5 × 56 × 13.5 cm. The inscription comes from the Castellaras de Mougins, where it was embedded in a wall next to an ancient chapel.
"To the Manes:
As you pass, look, I beg you, at this inscription
and you will weep! How prematurely I was robbed
by death, at age thirty; the gentle light of life
was taken from me, and, alone and childless,
I lived unhappily, and my poor mother has cried over me,
deprived of the honors of Filial piety.
For Quintus Luccunius Verus, her beloved son,
his mother Raiela Secundia has erected (this tomb)."

The patio portal opening onto the
Sculpture Garden.
Photo: Cuchi White.

78

View of the garden.
Photo: Lucarelli.

Abandoned like a sea shell on a strand, there are places whose passive magic lies in the fact that they have no purpose. Grimaldi Castle must have been such a place when Dor de la Souchère saw it for the first time. It was that strange magician Picasso who, inspired by the Museum's vacuity and — perhaps — its provincial charm, turned a medieval castle of uncertain style into a studio where he could give free rein to his power to transform — in function of his moods — the mythic or emotional reality he found in a special place. Dor de la Souchère made the first transformation possible, and understood the interest of presenting an artist's work in the environment that had inspired it. It remained — and still remains — to broaden this presentation by combining and developing its three principal components: Picasso and Antibes, Picasso and the artists of today, Grimaldi Castle and modern art.

Bibliography

The Picasso Donation
(Antibes 1981–1984)

Picasso's work in Antibes is reproduced in full in the six catalogues edited by Danièle Giraudy, the Curator of the Picasso Museum. They are published by the town of Antibes (the first four catalogues are currently being reprinted).

1. *L'Œuvre de Picasso à Antibes,* catalogue of the paintings, drawings, sculptures, ceramics, and tapestries in the Picasso Museum. Preface by Pierre Merli, introduction by Pierre Quoniam. 136 pages, 190 reproductions including 65 in color (1981).

2. *L'Œuvre de Picasso à Antibes,* the Centenary exhibition: Antibes, Juan-les-Pins, and Golfe-Juan from 1920 to 1946. 24 pages, 29 reproductions including 1 in color (1981).

3. *L'Œuvre de Picasso à Antibes,* catalogue of the engravings in the Picasso Museum.

View of the façade.

Preface by Pierre Merli. 64 pages, 50 reproductions including 1 in color (1982).

4. *A Travers Picasso,* a scientific study of the artist's technique, in collaboration with the Laboratory of the Museums of France. Preface by Pierre Merli, texts by Madeleine Hours, Christian Lahanier, Suzy Delbourgo, and Danièle Giraudy. 96 pages, 116 reproductions including 47 in color (1982).

5. *Bonjour Monsieur Picasso,* thirteen works commissioned for the tenth anniversary of Picasso's death: Adami, Alechinsky, Arman, Bioulès, César, Equipo Cronica, Erro, Folon, Guttuso, Messagier, Pignon, Raysse, Saura. 56 pages, 53 reproductions including 15 in color (1983).

6. *Picasso/tête à tête,* the sculptor's parable in an exhibition on the Museum's two monumental sculptures. Preface by Pierre Merli. 40 pages, 28 reproductions including 4 in color (1984).

Also by Danièle Giraudy:
Picasso, la mémoire du regard, le Cercle d'Art, Paris, 1986 (313 pages, 218 reproductions).

The Contemporary Art
Collections at
the Antibes Museum

7. *Catalogue raisonné du fonds d'art moderne du musée,* drawn up by Danièle Giraudy, published by the town of Antibes. Preface by Pierre Merli, texts by André Chastagnol, Georges Boudaille, and Georges Vindry. Introduction and history by Danièle Giraudy. Index of artists and works. 176 pages, 355 reproductions including 106 in color (1987).